Why God Made Colic

A First Time Mother's Journey

Penny-
Keep it REAL!.
Ronda

by: Ronda V. Paulson

Table of Contents

Acknowledgments

Thanks to my husband, Corey, for all your love and support. Words cannot express my gratitude. You are one of the greatest people I have ever met. I do not deserve you, but I thank God that He let me have you anyway.

Thanks to my daughter, Sophie, for without you there truly would be no book. You have changed my life in so many ways. You have made me see life more clearly, and I long to be a better person, thanks to you.

Thanks to my best friend, Brianna, for believing in me. Your encouragement from the treadmill means more than you will ever know. Thanks also for the concordance.

And finally, thanks to my mom and dad. Thank you for not giving me away when I had colic. More importantly though, thanks for loving me for the past 33 years, no matter how much I screamed and fussed.

Introduction

I was not an English major in college. I am not a writer nor have I ever had any desire to be a writer. But, before you put this book back on the shelf, allow me to explain. About two years ago, I felt God calling me to write a book. I chuckled at the idea (for all the reasons previously listed as well as many others). Try as I might to shake this absurd notion, the feeling only intensified. So here I am, two years and the birth of one daughter later, writing a book.

Six months ago, Sophia Ryan Paulson was born, and six months ago, my husband and I learned the term "colic." There is very little literature out there on the subject and even less support. We were entering into the abyss known as "colic" unprepared and uneducated. The only information our pediatrician gave us was the following definition: "colic - unexplained crying exceeding 6 hours a day." Needless to say, we had already figured that much out. My mother tried to be helpful, but for the most part, she would just shake her head as if experiencing some sort of post war trauma and say, "Oh Ronda, it was awful. You had it, and it was awful!" We longed for an explanation, an answer, something! So now, six months later, as a "colic" survivor, I am ready to help all those parents who have been given nothing but a definition and a pat on the back. I want to reach out to those who have been told good luck by some pediatrician as he rushed them out the door. I want to say there is hope and even humor in your colic predicament if you will allow God to show you the way.

Why God Made Colic is obviously a book for those who

have had children with colic or are currently experiencing what it means to have a colicky baby. <u>Why God Made Colic</u> is also for anyone who has ever experienced God helping them grow in a not so pleasant manner. It is a book that will hopefully make you laugh, cry, and most importantly, ponder some of the tough questions. It is a book of hope, love, and God's mercy for us all. So sit back, relax, and enjoy reading a book by an author of whom you have never heard, letting God take care of the rest.

Chapter One
What Have We Done?

December 26

    I had four fairly simple prayer requests surrounding the birth of our daughter: 1) Please, let our baby arrive safely, 2) Please, help me not be mean to my husband during delivery, 3) Please, allow my in-laws (who were traveling from Indiana) time to get to the hospital, and 4) If possible, please, let my hair be fixed, toe-nails and fingernails be painted, and my legs be clean shaven. I really did not consider this too much to ask. The past nine months had been no picnic, and God knew what a trooper I had been. I mean honestly, if You can create the universe in six days, then what are four little prayer requests? Well, as usual, God came through for me. He answered all of my prayer requests. On December 23, the doctor informed my husband and me that I would need a C-section, which was promptly scheduled for December 26. So, here I am. Nails painted, legs shaved, feeling no urge to speak harshly to my husband, and waiting for them to deliver my baby as safely as possible - they are just going to go get her. No trauma to her little head, no chance of shoulders getting stuck, no umbilical cord dilemmas, just lifting her out. It is at times like this that you realize God does have a sense of humor. I just wonder sometimes how often God smiles to Himself as I pray some self absorbed, "I deserve this" prayer. I envision Him shaking His head and thinking, "When will she ever learn?" And then He reaches down and helps His child, even though she does not deserve anything.

    So that's it. That is how it happened. I know nothing of water breaking, contractions, or dilation. All I know is that at 11:30 AM, a nurse walked in and said, "Let's go get that baby." At approximately 12:30 PM, a needle was injected into my back. And the next words I hear are, "Go get the husband; we have started the incision." My husband entered swiftly into the room, sat down beside me, and pushed his head close to mine. It was at that moment I knew he would whisper words of love and gratitude. He would take these final moments before the birth of our daughter to thank me for carrying our child, for loving him, and for being a wonderful partner. He moved in closer and began to chant over and over again in my ear, "I'm not looking. I'm not looking. I'm not looking." He stopped only briefly when the doctor called out, "O.K. Dad, look over the curtain," to which he answered with great resolve, "I'M NOT LOOKING!"

The next sound in the room was one I had dreamed of for 9 months. At 12:58 PM, our daughter let out her first cry. It was music to our ears. We could not believe it. Just moments ago, she had been inside me, and now she was in the world, taking in oxygen, feeling cold air for the first time, being touched by human hands, all of which was making her very mad. But we didn't care. We loved the crying! Our hearts jumped for joy at the crying! We wanted the crying to go on and on. Little did we know - it would.

The next few hours were a blur. I remember lying in the recovery area thinking, "Where is my baby?!" I had waited 9 months to see my child, and all I got was a glimpse of her face as they left the room with her. Now, as the rest of my family watched her through a window, and as her father (who, for any of you that may need reminding of this, DID NOT carry her for the past nine months) touched her and video taped her every move, I lay in recovery, listening to two nurses discuss where their next pay checks would be going. Sometimes, life does not seem fair. However, after what seemed like an eternity, I was wheeled back to my room, and Sophia was placed in my arms.

This is the point in the story that I wish I could paint a beautiful picture for you of a mother seeing her child for the first time. I wish I could write words that would make you misty eyed and feel warm and fuzzy inside. I'm sure time has a way of changing these first moments into just that, a beautiful, life-altering, miraculous event. But for now - I have to be honest - I was in shock. I just kept staring at this baby they had handed me. I knew I was supposed to feel all of these maternal emotions, but I just kept staring at what appeared to be my husband's clone. I had given birth to a female Corey Paulson! How could this be?! I was the one who had gained 52 pounds. I was the one with the stretch marks. I was the one wearing a size 40 DD nursing bra. I was the one with the incision. And my husband, looking as cute as ever, just walked around the hospital room in his "Awesome Dad" visor, beaming. He was smiling from ear to ear as everyone said, "She looks just like you." God, You are a funny, funny Divine Being! A funny, funny Divine Being!

December 27

Breast feeding is rocket science! Any woman who tries to describe her initial experience with breast feeding as anything else has either forgotten or she is lying. Contrary to popular belief, it is not a time of relaxation and bonding. It is not natural or beautiful. It is rocket science. I have never been a free spirit when it comes to nudity. I am not one to willingly expose myself and, in many ways, believe there is something to be said for modesty - but not on December 27th. Anyone who was willing to help me saw my breast. Why? Because, as stated above, breast feeding is rocket science. There are positioning, head holding techniques, "let down," redness, soreness, and yes, even scabbing over of an area I thought incapable of scabbing over. There is the need for the application of ointments, tea bags, and cold cabbage leaves. Also, everyone is asking, "Has your milk come in yet?" My response, "How am I supposed to know?" Their response, "Oh, you'll know. You'll know." What?

Needless to say, at this point, I am a little stressed. My day began with my husband bathing me. Now before you get the wrong idea, allow me to explain. I had to lift my stretch mark covered stomach, which was hanging over my new incision, so that Corey could inspect the area. I know he was thinking, "What happened to the woman I married," even though the words were never said. I'm still not used to this kid for whom I am supposed to feel overwhelming love. And to make matters even worse, the nurse keeps bringing her to me and sticking her to my chest. My room is full of people, and honestly, I can barely keep my eyes open because I do not handle medication well. The highlight of my day was when a nurse stopped by and said that the nursing staff had decided I had the prettiest baby in the nursery. Later, I would find out that there was only Sophie and one other baby, a 10 pound female with an extremely large cone head. I was, exhausted, guilt-ridden, and in pain. However, after watching my husband's first attempt to change Sophie's diaper, I had enough mothers' intuition about me to know that if this kid was going to make it, if my marriage was going to make it, Mama had better buck up!

December 28

Things were looking up. I discussed my medication with my nurse and decided that I was tired of being out of it. So for the next few hours, I had nothing but over the counter pain medication and I was feeling the fog begin to lift. I took a shower by myself. Side note: I decided that it would be a very long time before my husband saw me naked again. But aside from just starting to feel like Ronda, something else was happening. I found myself thinking about the "kid" more. I got out of the shower wondering what my little one was doing in the nursery. By the time I was ready, I wanted Corey to go get her. I longed to see that little face. Even at 3:30 this morning, when I heard her cry coming down the hall, I found myself a little excited about getting to spend time with her - pain and all. We were becoming acquaintances - you know, the kind of acquaintance to whom you feel connected because she knew your mother or because you are best friends with her best friend's brother's girlfriend - a kind of familiarity and common bond even though you just met.

I already know her cry as she travels toward me.
And I know she likes the bigger boob
(Who doesn't?).
I know how she feels right before she falls asleep on my breast
Because she would rather sleep than eat.
There is still a lot of awkwardness,
As there is with any new relationship,
But there is definitely a closeness that I like.
I like it when she is near me.
I think about her when she is not.
She makes me smile even though I am still tired and sore.

Now I don't want to rush it,
But I think we may have something here.
I know it has only been two days,
But I think
I'm falling for her.

December 29

Well, it is here, the day we take our daughter home. The day we leave the hospital and the nursing staff and take over full responsibility for the welfare and survival of our first born. It is actually a little hard to believe. I mean, there is a nurse who knows nothing about me or my husband handing me a sheet of paper with what she describes as some general care instructions. She also mentions that she will need to see the car seat in the car before we leave - and that's it. That's it? One sheet of instructions and a safe ride home and we are on our own, on our own to feed, clothe, bathe, and raise a morally sound and giving member of society. That's right folks -they'll let anybody be a parent - even me. I knew this day was coming, but I was not prepared for the overwhelming feeling of aloneness. Sure, my mother is right here, and I made it. Corey's mother is right here, and he made it. But I can't help but feel the weight of this enormous responsibility on my shoulders. It probably isn't helping that Corey keeps asking me what to do. I want to scream, "HOW SHOULD I KNOW!" It is as if he has forgotten that he is the only man to whom I have ever been married and that this is OUR first child.

As we travel down the hall for her first photograph, you know the one we all have taken by a nurse as we lay in a bassinet, Sophie begins to cry. Over the past few days, we were beginning to realize she wasn't the happiest of babies. I mean, she slept quite a bit, but she also stayed awake quite a bit. And she didn't always seem comfortable. She acted like her stomach hurt. The nurses suggested Mylicon Drops but they really didn't seem to help. For the moment, Sophie was mad. Sophie stayed mad during the pictures, the final paper work, and the introduction to the car seat, and the final mini conference with our nurse. And by the way, during our conference, the nurse asked if my milk had come in!? By the time we reached the car, I was a mess! There was sweat dripping from everywhere. My incision was killing me because I had been on my feet for the past three hours, and did I mention that Sophie was not happy? That's right - still crying. For those of you who may have forgotten what is was like to be around a screaming baby for any length of time, I liken it to the worst headache ever. You know the kind of headache that you can't seem to get rid of, the kind of headache that makes you incapable of thinking clearly. The kind of headache that robs you of clear judgment and that makes you hateful and cranky. That is what Corey and I experienced as we drove home. Sophie could not be comforted. We had no idea how common this helpless feeling would become over the next few months. For now, I tried to remain calm and reassure Corey that babies cry and that she was probably hungry. I reminded him that there are car seat safety laws and that I would get her out and feed her as soon as we got home. We drove the rest of the way in silence - well, except for Sophie.

The rest of the afternoon was more of the same. Sophie would cry, I would feed her, she would sleep. The house was full of family, and my friend Brianna brought over dinner. I do not remember anything after dinner until about 11:00 PM. It was around this time that our night really began.

At 11:00 PM, Sophie began to cry. Corey and I had decided to camp out on the couch while Sophie slept in her bassinet. We were all sleeping in the den because we did not want to bother Corey's mom and dad who were sleeping upstairs. At least we WERE all sleeping until 11:00 PM. As I said, Sophie began to cry. Corey lifted her out of her bassinet and changed her diaper as I began to get everything ready to feed her. This ritual had been going on for the past few days, and even though we were no longer in the confines of the hospital, there was something about the familiar that made everything feel safe. Corey handed her to me and lay down to go back to sleep. However, this time Sophie did not stop crying when she reached my chest. As a matter of fact, she cried harder as I attempted to feed her. Corey began to frantically ask, "What's wrong? Why is she still crying? Why isn't she eating?"

I don't know, I thought. I had known this kid for four days and for four days if she cried I stuck her to my chest and she stopped. I found myself puzzled, perplexed. I also found myself ignoring my husband who was still pacing back and forth in his underwear, asking question after question. I knew I couldn't let him know I was scared. I had learned in a few short days that daddies need to know that mommies have it all under control. But I didn't have it all under control. I had no idea what to do. And he could see it in my eyes. Like a dog, he smelled fear, and it made him very uncomfortable.

The scene remained the same until about 2:30. From 11:00 PM to 2:30 AM, I would walk Sophie around the den as she cried, trying not to bump into my husband, in his underwear, as he walked around the den asking questions. I would stop periodically to try to feed her, but this only angered her more. For 2 ½ hours, I put on my "It is O.K." face, but inside, I was dying! How could I not be able to feed my child? What was I doing wrong? I knew she was hungry - she had to be! She was hungry and confused as to why this woman who had done a pretty good job up until now would not feed her. On top of all of this, my in-laws were upstairs. I didn't want them to know that I was incapable of breast feeding my child and that I could not calm her down. I didn't want them to know that I was failing as a mother, and I had only had her home for about 10 hours. And above all else, I did not want to ask for help. I mean what kind of mother would that makes me? I had to do this on my own.

Until 2:30 AM! I lost it! I absolutely lost it! I handed the kid over to my husband and began to cry. Needless to say, Corey did not handle this well. He began to cry. That's right, Corey in his underwear, me with my boob hanging out, and Sophie in her "Happy Girl" sleeper - just crying and crying and crying. We all cried off and on until about 5:00 AM. Sophie cried because she was hungry, tired, and the hospital had let two crazy people take her home. Corey cried because as a man he wanted to fix the situation, and he couldn't. And me, I cried because I had failed. I had always been pretty good at just about anything I put my mind to. If I tried hard enough, I could fix just about every predicament I got myself into. But not this time, I was tired, hurting, and too full of pride to ask for help. After hours of trying to pretend, I had failed, so I cried. We all fell asleep around 5:00 AM - tired, hungry, frustrated, and confused.

They say that everything is better in the light of day. Ha! I would like to have invited "they" over the next morning. Around 8:00 AM, Sophie began to cry. Of course she did. For those of you keeping track, it has been almost 12 hours since my newborn had a good meal. I was at a loss. I could not understand why she would not eat. She would not even latch on. And then it came to me, like a revelation, a dream, a vision - God was punishing me. Why hadn't I realized it earlier? After all my jokes about breast feeding being barbaric, after all my comments about the dog next door and me having entirely too much in common, feeding our young with our "teats" and all. After complaining about the pain and the complexity of what is supposed to be a natural thing - God was punishing me. He had decided to show me that He was sick and tired of all my whining, and therefore, I would no longer be given the option of breast feeding. Well, it was like telling a dieter that she couldn't have chocolate. What do you mean not breast feed? I must breast feed! I long to breast feed! I will just die if I can't breast feed! At 8:30 AM, I gave up all hope and asked Corey to call my friend Brianna and ask how much formula a newborn should eat. I cried as I said the words, and I began to cry harder as I heard the words spoken on the phone. Corey was still choked up as well, and between Sophie and me crying in the background and Corey crying on the phone, Brianna said she would be right over.

Just like old friends do, Brianna and I started crying all over again when we saw each other. Brianna had just calmed me down when she asked, "Has your milk come in yet?" Wrong question, I cried harder than ever. "I don't know," I sobbed. Didn't anyone understand? I was a breast feeding failure. I was no longer worthy of the breasts pregnancy had given me. But Brianna had the answer to all our questions: the breast pump. Brianna reassured me that it was O.K. and that not every woman knows when her milk comes in. At this point, I did not know if she was just lying to make me feel better, you know, like saying, "No, your butt doesn't look big," but I didn't care. I did feel better, at least until I saw the breast pump. "You want me to do what?" I asked. But I had not been mistaken. She wanted me to stick my breasts into a sucking apparatus and push start. She also thought it would be a good idea to turn up the suction just to make sure it would work. Brianna must have seen the fear and confusion in my eyes and without hesitation, she did the only thing a best friend could do; she did it for me. That's right. I am sitting in our leather recliner with my stomach and breasts exposed. Brianna is positioned on the floor between my legs holding the dual fisted torture device and leaning in to make sure that the machine is properly PULLING my utters. It was at that moment I began to laugh. I had not laughed in days. I began to laugh, Brianna began to laugh, and milk began to flow. MY MILK WAS IN! To all those people who had answered me with a slow, drawn out "You'll know. You'll know," I didn't. I had no idea. Nothing had changed. There was no tingling, rapid growth, or leakage. And no one had said anything to me about a word that is now burned into my memory - engorgement. My milk had come in, and my breasts were so full that Sophie could not latch on. We pumped, fed Sophie a bottle, and made an appointment with Melanie, a lactation consultant. We all hugged Brianna as she left, even the in-laws.

Spending the afternoon with Melanie was quite an experience. A woman I had never met before, after a brief introduction, asked me to bare my breast and proceeded to grab it from me. In a few short minutes, my breast was being lifted toward the ceiling, and Sophie's head was being forced upon it. And that was it. Sophie was eating. While she ate, Melanie explained to me that my nipple was "flimsy" and that I would need to place it properly in order for Sophie to nurse. She also informed me that my five day old daughter knew how she liked her meals, and if I did not fix her dinner exactly the way she wanted it, she would not eat. Melanie left the room while Sophie ate and said that she would return to watch me position the second breast. As I sat there in the hospital room, I was filled with emotion. My daughter was nursing again, and I was so thankful. For the first time, I understood the bonding and relaxation other women had described. As I sat there basking in my womanhood, proud to be a mother, and enjoying the closeness of my child, I caught a glimpse for the first time of how a father's love is different from a mother's love. We had been up all night. Our daughter had practically starved to death, and I was frantic about not being able to breast feed. And now that everything seemed to be working out, my husband leaned in and asked, "How many breasts you think she sees a day?" In the middle of this beautiful moment, my husband was sitting across the room with what I thought to be a smile of contentment and relief. Come to find out, the smile was actually an outward expression of his inward contemplation of a new career. My husband was trying to figure out how he could become a lactation specialist while I was intently listening to how we were going to save our daughter's life. Like I said, there is a difference between a father's and a mother's love.

As we rode home, I realized that it had been days since I had prayed. I was in the middle of the single most miraculous experience of my life, and I had not been praying. I made up all kinds of excuses in my head, but the bottom line was I had not thanked God for the beautiful, healthy baby that was riding in our backseat. I was ashamed. How could I ask for God's help when I had not even thanked Him for this wonderful gift? So I decided I could not possibly ask God for help. Instead, I spent the rest of the day thanking Him for giving us Sophie.

The next few days all kind of blurred into one. My in-laws left for Indiana, and although my heart was breaking for my mother-in-law because I knew she did not want to leave her first grandchild, I was happy to see them go. I was glad to see them go but not for the reasons most women would be glad to see their mother-in-law go. You see, I love Mary Jane very much. She is a wonderful woman, and she has always treated me like a daughter, not a daughter-in-law. I was glad to see them go because I was tired of faking it. I was so tired of acting happy when I wasn't. I was so tired of acting like I had it all together when I didn't. And mostly, I was tired of all the effort it was taking not to sit down and have a good cry. You see, since the engorgement night, I hadn't cried. I had walked around like my incision wasn't hurting, doing my best not to ask for help. Sophie was my responsibility, and it would not be fair to burden anyone else.

Visitors would come and go. People would bring in food and say things like, "Isn't motherhood wonderful?" Did these women suffer from amnesia? Had they blocked out the first days of their children's lives? Or worse, was I doing something wrong? I was not experiencing wonderful. I was experiencing sleep deprivation. This, of course, is not how I would answer them. I would smile and say, "Yes," and fuss at Corey for saying things like, "I don't know. I didn't realize there would be so much crying." I would long for them to leave because I was tired of faking it. But each time they left, Corey and I would be staring at one another not saying much of anything. For anyone who knows us, this is not normal behavior. Corey and I are extremely close and very much in tune with one another. But not this time, we were cranky and hateful with one another and when other people weren't around, not much was said at all. There was a distance that was very uncomfortable, the kind of distance that hangs over two people who are keeping something from one another. I longed for the distance to be gone, but I could not tell him my secret.

As for Sophie, she was becoming increasingly unhappy. We did not know what to do. There would be moments of crying in which nothing seemed to appease her, and then there would be moments of bliss. I would become quite mean when Corey would insinuate that there might be something wrong. "No, Corey," I would say, "She's a baby and babies cry!" But was there something wrong? She did seem uncomfortable at times. None of our parenting classes had said anything about the enormous or what we thought at the time was enormous, amounts of crying. She was supposed to eat and sleep. We would hear people comment on how bright eyed she was. They would say things like, "I don't think we saw little Johnny's eyes until he was about three months old." Not Sophie. She was bright eyed and ready to go. When we went to the doctor, all the other babies were asleep in their carriers. They seemed lethargic and uninterested in the world around them. Not Sophie. She sat in the waiting room, eyes wide open and screaming at the top of her lungs. Corey and I began to think that maybe the other parents drugged their children. Then we began to wonder where we could find that drug.

All of this tension and confusion continued to fester until January 5. Corey was to leave town for Phoenix the next day. It was probably a combination of everything I stated above with a little bit of resentment. This was the man who got me in this mess, and now he was now leaving on a business trip to a resort in Arizona. The pot finally boiled over. When all was said and done, Corey and I were sitting on the couch crying and ashamed. The secret that had put so much distance between us was out in the open. God had given us this beautiful baby girl, and we were looking at each other, both of us asking, what have we done? We had a good life! We loved each other. We went out to eat. We sat and watched T.V. We had sex. We slept in. We laughed. What had we done? We could not believe how self-centered we were being. We felt guilty that the thoughts were even there. I mean, how unappreciative could two people be? But that's where we were, on a couch, crying, wondering if life would ever be the same again. If not the same, would it at least be fun? Fun? We'd settle for tolerable. Our conversation ended with Sophie starting to cry. Just like before, Corey got up to go get her and change her diaper, and I got everything ready to feed her. For the moment, Sophie needed us, and our discussion would have to wait.

Chapter Two
Dad Leaves Town
And
All "Colic"
Breaks Loose

DAY 1

The morning of January 6 Corey was scheduled to leave for Phoenix. The trip had been planned since October, and after much debate, we decided that he should go. We were both a little leery about him leaving, but since I was tossing around the idea of not returning to work, it seemed more important than ever that he keep his boss happy. Corey left around 6:00 AM and my mother arrived around 9:00 AM. Being the wonderful mother that she is, she had taken a week of vacation to stay with Sophie and me. I can only imagine her expectations for the week. I'm sure that she thought, as I did, that it would be a fun week for just us girls, the kind of week in which special memories are made, the kind of memories you discuss at family get-togethers for years to come. I have now titled this the "what were we thinking" phase.

Sophie lay back down around 8:30 AM, and when mom arrived, we ate breakfast together and talked about our day. It was around 11:00 AM, and I had just decided to take a shower, when Sophie began to cry. Mom offered to get her, but I said that she was probably hungry so I would feed her first. As she ate, she seemed increasingly more and more uncomfortable. After she ate, it was as if she needed to burp but couldn't. Even after she finally did burp, she seemed miserable, and everyone knows what miserable babies do - they cry! Sophie began to cry. I walked, patted, bounced, and whispered "Shh, shh, shh," over and over again, none of which seemed to soothe the little one. I could feel my anxiety level rising. I did not know what to do. Mom remained surprisingly calm. This is very uncharacteristic of our relationship. Over the years, while I would remain surprisingly calm, my mother was a different story. But for now, I was the stressed out new mom, and she was the experienced mother with pearls of wisdom to share, the first little gem being that Sophie was getting tired and probably just had gas. That is when my mother pulled me into the "I'm sure this will pass" phase. Mom took over and began to walk and pat and bounce and "shh." Nothing. Sophie continued to cry.

We quickly entered the "check list" phase. Is her diaper wet? Check. Is she hot? Check. Is she cold? Check. Does she have a fever? Check. Is she hungry? Check. Did we try the Mylicon Drops? Check. Well then, she must be tired. I mean, she is only 10 days old, and she has now been awake for almost an hour. She must be tired. She has to be tired. So we walked, patted, bounced, and whispered, "Shh-shh-shh," one after the other. I would go first and continue the ritual until I was to the point of crying myself. Mom would take over and continue the ritual until I felt guilt or she had nicotine fit. This went on until Sophie's next feeding 3 ½ hours later.

Next, we entered the "denial" phase. We had been denying the colic possibility for the past two weeks, and now, locked in this house together, we would not even entertain the idea. It was not colic. No, no. In fact, it was very simple. Sophie was a newborn, and newborns need lots of sleep. Sophie was fighting sleep, and after her next feeding, we were sure that she would just give up the fight. Denial, denial, denial!

After her next feeding, we hit the "what are we going to do we are losing our minds" phase. You see, Sophie didn't just give up the fight. My newborn had now been awake for almost five hours and showed no signs of drifting off to sleep any time soon. She had been crying for five hours. We had been walking, bouncing, patting, "shh"-ing, and racking our brains for five hours. We were about to crack! I was about to take up smoking, and it was obvious that Mom was having flash backs to when I had colic. She had told me stories over the years, stories of her walking around the house for hours while I cried stories of how she would have done anything to make me happy. She had even contemplated giving me to a neighbor who stopped by because I stopped crying when she took me. Every time she told these stories, she got the same far away look in her eye and began to twitch slightly. She would then close her eyes and shake her head as if to brush off the horrible memories as quickly as possible. She had that same look in her eye now as she walked around the living room. She even had a slight twitch, and I could hear her mumbling, "Surely not, surely not."

In the middle of the "what are we going to do we are losing our minds" phase, my husband called. Now, just to refresh your memory, when Corey left, Sophie was asleep, and although she had been increasingly cranky, other than the engorgement night, she had been consolable. My husband left a mildly fussy baby with his seemingly sane wife, and that is who he thought he was calling. Mom answered the phone. I could hear her saying, "It's not good. Things aren't going so well." In my mind, I knew what Corey was thinking. He was saying to himself, "My mother-in-law is a little on the dramatic side; just let me speak to my clear minded, stable wife." Mom handed me the phone, and as soon as Corey said, "How are things?" I started to cry. My husband, feeling guilty about not being there, did what any man would do when he feels guilty - he got hateful. "Ronda, I'm sorry! You told me to go! It will be O.K.! Don't make me feel bad! What can I do? Tell me what to do!"

"Nothing," I sobbed. "We're fine," sniff, sniff.

"Just go have a good time. I'm sure she'll stop crying eventually." Corey said he had to go, and I got off the phone feeling guilty for not being able to keep it together. Corey got off the phone confused. Where was his wife? How could things possibly be that bad? Would he actually have been better off just talking to his mother-in-law? He did not realize that we were not being dramatic. We were both in the middle of the "what are we going to do we are losing our minds" phase, and there was no way to reason with or have a civilized conversation with either one of us.

Next came the "what could it hurt" phase. This phase started with my mother running an empty dishwasher. She was standing in front of the dishwasher, bouncing and patting while Sophie listened to the clangs and whooshes. I must have been looking at my mother with a puzzled expression because she whispered, "I read this in an article once. The sound is supposed to soothe a crying baby. What could it hurt?" Surprisingly enough, it seemed to be working. There we all were in the kitchen, my mother in her sweat pants and no make up, swaying Sophie back in forth in front of a dishwasher with no dishes in it, and me in my pajamas watching the whole thing finding it hard to believe that it was now 6:00 PM. Sophie caught a cat nap and was ready to go again by about 6:20. "Want to try bathing her?" my mother suggested. "I read in an article once that a warm bath is soothing. What could it hurt?" So we tried a bath. She hated it! My mother then suggested a drive. "Some babies like the car. What could it hurt?" Sophie hated the car. Mom then suggested sitting her on top of the dryer. I mean, what could it hurt? Well, probably a lot, considering that we have no heat in our basement and it was about 23 degrees outside. We decided to rule out that option. "Maybe we should try some more Mylicon Drops," I said. Mom answered, "What could it hurt?" By now, Sophie laughed in the face of Mylicon Drops. She would swallow the drops, pause, almost grin, and then begin to scream louder than ever. At 3:30 AM we tried our last trick. Sophie had been crying since 11:00 AM on January 6. It was now 3:30 AM on January 7. I know that seems hard to believe. I was there, and it seems hard to believe. But it is all true. My newborn had been crying for almost 17 hours. Needless to say, when my mother suggested that we turn on the vacuum cleaner, I figured, what could it hurt? Down deep I will have to admit I thought she was crazy. I thought, "Love her. She has finally lost it. No cigarettes, no food, nothing to drink, no shower, no sleep, she has finally lost it." Mom plugged in the vacuum at 3:45 AM. By 3:46 AM, Sophie was out cold. It was almost instant. It was a miracle. Sophie was screaming, vacuum cleaner clicked on, Sophie's head fell down on my mother's shoulder, and she was out! We just looked at each other in amazement. She was sleeping. She was actually sleeping. After a moment of basking in the quiet and after pausing to thank God for the invention of the vacuum, we quickly laid her down and got ready for bed. Mom took her position on the living room couch, or so I thought. And I, with Sophie and the vacuum cleaner by my side, took my position on the couch in the den. I was just about to drift off to sleep to the peaceful, rhythmic hum of our Hoover when I heard a knock at the door. It is 4:00 AM! Who could possibly be knocking at the door? As I rounded the corner, I could see a shadow on the front porch. There was a hooded silhouette on my front porch at 4:00 AM! I would have been really scared except for the fact that, other than the somewhat menacing looking hood, the stranger was only about 5 feet tall and appeared to be of small stature. And that's when I realized who it was. I was now standing at the front door looking out at my mother. Love her. She had gone outside, in her winter coat, hood and all, with her

Frappucino, to smoke. In her sleep deprived state, she had locked herself out. We both laughed as we looked at each other. I unlocked the door and just walked away shaking my head. We both finally lay down at 4:15 AM and giggled ourselves to sleep. This was going to be a week of special memories alright, the kind of memories you discuss at family get-togethers for years to come.

DAY 3

Sophie woke up around 8:00 AM, and thus began day three. Sophie would eat, become miserable, be inconsolable for about 3 hours, fall asleep for 30 minutes to an hour (only if she was being held, you could not lay her down), and wake up ready to go again. My mother and I had not showered in almost 48 hours, and needless to say, tensions were pretty high. We were not eating, not sleeping, not showering. We were, however, doing a lot of walking, bouncing, patting you know the drill. Once again, my husband called. Each time he called, I knew he wanted me to lie and say things were fine. I knew he wanted to be reassured that he had done the right thing by leaving us. I also knew that he wanted me not to cry on the phone because it made him feel helpless. But you know I really didn't care what he wanted. Not to sound cold or calloused, but my husband was in Phoenix, at a resort hotel, eating shrimp the size of his head, and having a wonderful time. I was stuck in a house with a screaming baby and my mother, who I had to start watching a little more closely after the whole front porch incident. I was lucky to get my teeth brushed and go to the bathroom. Corey was eating the chocolates off his pillow before going to bed, while I was walking laps around our dining room, listening to a vacuum cleaner. I'll be honest; I was a little bitter. Between being bitter and just being tired, I was not very nice when I answered the phone. "Hello," I said. "Hi. How are things going?"

How are things going? How are things going? How do you think things are going? I simply replied, "Fine."

"How's Sophie?" Corey asked.

How's Sophie? Crazy! Miserable! Inconsolable!

Screaming her head off! "She's not happy," I said.

"Ronda, what am I supposed to do?"

"I don't know, Corey!" We never called each other by our first names.

Then Corey said something I will never forget, "Maybe I just shouldn't call anymore?"

"What?!?!" How could he say that? Not call? I needed him. Didn't he understand that? I needed to hear his voice. I needed to know he cared. I needed him to understand how important he was to my sanity. So I answered the only way I knew how. "Oh, that's a great idea! Yeah, if I were you I just wouldn't bother calling to check on the LOVE of YOUR LIFE and YOUR NEWBORN DAUGHTER!"

Corey's rebuttal was just as hateful as he answered, "I can't take this!"

"You know what I can't take, Corey? I can't take you having the audacity to be hateful to me when I am losing my mind! I don't have time to poop, so I surely don't have time for you to be hateful!" Slam, went the phone! Where was all this coming from? I don't talk to my husband like this. That is not the way I intended that conversation to go. What was wrong with me?

What was wrong was that my life had no resemblance of my old life. My body was stretched, scarred, flabby, and tired. My house was a wreck. I had no job. I couldn't even go to church. My husband was out of town. And worst of all, my beautiful baby girl was miserable, and I couldn't help her. I was exhausted both mentally and physically. I was confused and borderline depressed. I had never had such little control over a situation in my life. I needed God, but I felt guilty praying. I felt like I was just being weak, and all I really needed to do was just suck it up. The only person I could take all of this out on was Corey. I expected him to understand everything I was going through even though he was thousands of miles away and, honestly, I didn't even understand it myself.

The "it" I didn't understand now had a name. Denial was over. My baby had colic or "The Colic" as we east Tennesseans like to call it. Sophie's colic started on January 6, and by January 8, I was going insane. The really sad part of the whole thing is colic usually lasts for 3 months. How would we ever make it through?

There was a knock at the door around 4:00 PM, and a man delivered a beautiful bouquet of flowers. The card read, "Hang in there. Love, Corey." I smiled as I put the card back in the envelope. "I am married to a good man," I thought. I also thought, "He's right. I just need to hang in there." Sophie started screaming in the background, hanging in there would be easier said than done.

DAY 4

By this time, Mom and I had a system - well sort of. Mom would answer all phone calls and say that Sophie and I were sleeping. This, of course, was a complete lie, but I didn't have the energy to be cordial. People would stop by, bringing food, wanting to see the baby. They would always ask how things were going, so we would tell them Sophie had colic, and she was very fussy. To those visitors who had never experienced colic themselves, you could see it in their eyes - we were just whining about the natural adjustment period of becoming a mother. But, to those visitors who had experienced colic, there was an instant connection, a bond, a secret sisterhood. You could see empathy in their eyes. You could see a longing to help in what they knew to be a helpless situation. You could also see fear. It was as if they must grab their child and leave at once for fear that their now 13 year old would become colicky all over again. When visitors weren't around, Mom and I would take turns caring for Sophie. We had learned that you must carry her upright at all times. She hated the sound of the human voice when she was upset, so singing or talking sweetly were definite no-no's. She liked to be held tightly, bounced up and down hard, patted on the back with a firm, rhythmic pat, and when all else failed, turn on the Hoover. Mom would shower while I walked, and then I would shower. We made a pact that when someone was in the shower she was not to be bothered. You see, it was a safe haven. With the vent on and the water running, you could not hear the cry of a colic-driven baby. It was a little piece of heaven in the midst of what can only be described as hell. Mom wasn't always good at keeping the pact. I know she would secretly move closer and closer to the door. If I didn't respond, she would crack the door and say, "I think your daughter needs you" or "She's awake." Even though she wasn't good at keeping our pact, she had been wonderful at everything else. My mother had been so helpful, and it felt so safe with her beside me. I didn't want her to ever leave.

Mom was leaving, though, that very night, as a matter of fact. Corey was to arrive home around 9:30 PM, and then mom was going home. All day long, I could feel my fears growing. I loved the safety of our routine. I loved that she knew all Sophie's little quirks. I was still mad, subconsciously, at Corey for going on a trip I told him to go on, and now he was coming home, and mom was leaving. Poor Corey, as he walked through the door, awaiting a warm welcome, I gave him the cold shoulder and went into the bedroom. My mom and Corey both followed me, and I began to cry. Mom offered to stay, and as much as I wanted her to, I had to tell her to go. My husband and I needed to deal with our daughter together. We needed to work as a team, and that would not happen as long as mom stayed. As she left, I could feel a lump in my throat again. I knew I needed to be a grown-up, but I longed just to be her little girl again and let her fix everything like she had so many times before. I knew I needed to be a mother and, more importantly, a wife. I knew it was time, but I was scared. I was so scared and, at this point, very disillusioned. Motherhood had not been anything I expected it to be. My daughter was miserable and cried all the time. She seemed to hate life, and she seemed to hate me. I wasn't expecting it to be easy, but I was expecting a little enjoyment here and there. Right now, enjoyment was taking a shower, and reality was knowing that as soon as I turned off the water, Sophie would be crying.

Corey was quickly initiated into the hidden world of

the colic. He just couldn't understand. "Why does she keep crying?" he would ask.

"Because she has colic," was my response. Over and over again, we would say these words. I taught Corey the official "Sophie" hold and gave him the run down on what we had found to be effective and what was not. Initially, he was very hesitant concerning the vacuum cleaner. Corey was still in the mindset of a parent with a normal child. We had taken a parenting class which had given us all kinds of helpful advice. The class materials suggested not rocking your child to sleep, not letting your child have any "sleep props" (things that help them fall asleep), etc. We continued to argue over how best to help Sophie. I stayed calm this time, however, because after all, I had been with Sophie all week; Corey had not. I had come to the decision to throw our parenting class book out the window, and I knew he would soon make that decision for himself. And he did. At 4:30 AM, Corey picked our daughter up out of her bassinet, held her tightly in the "Sophie" position, bounced and patted her back, as he made his way quickly over to the vacuum cleaner, which he proceeded to kick on. Sophie drifted off to sleep, and he sat down on the couch beside me.

"So this is what you have been doing all week?"

"Yes," I said.

"I had no idea," he said.

"I know," I said.

"I'm sorry."

"I know, I know." And that is how our first week with the colic ended, Corey, sitting up at the end of our sectional, holding Sophie as he slept. I fell asleep, sitting up on the other end of the couch, lights on, T.V. on, and of course, the vacuum cleaner running.

Chapter Three
What is
"The Colic"?

DAY 5

We were back in our doctor's office bright and early Friday morning. Corey came home Thursday night, spent one evening with our colic-driven, screaming angel and had all of us in the doctor's office first thing the next day. "I just don't get it, Ronda! What is colic? How do we know there is not something else wrong with our child?" Corey asked these questions and variations of these questions over and over again as we drove to our appointment. I sat in the passenger seat, numb. I had already spent four days asking these same questions. I just kept thinking that maybe our pediatrician would shed some new light on our situation.

Dr. Thathelpsalot (or so we will call him) entered the room with a warm grin and a friendly, "How's everybody doing this morning?" As if on cue, Sophie began to cry. I felt the now very familiar lump begin to rise in my throat, and Corey "Mr. Question" Paulson clammed up.

I finally muttered, "Not real good," and began to cry. Corey took over. He explained how Sophie would eat, become very uncomfortable and gassy, and cry until her next feeding. He put great emphasis on the fact that this cycle would continue from 7:00 AM to 3:00 AM THE NEXT DAY! After examining Sophie, our doctor diagnosed her with colic. He said that most colicky babies, like Sophie, are healthy and continue to gain weight. He reassured us that there were no signs of failure to thrive and that she appeared fine, minus the hours upon hours of inconsolable crying. Dr. Thathelpsalot thought that we should look at the positive. Our baby was completely healthy and growing just beautifully. He handed us a sheet of paper with a brief definition of colic, and then he turned to me. He looked me straight in the eye and told me that it was very important for me to get out of the house for a little while. He also gave me a number to call in case my frustration level got so high that I thought I might injure my child. Lastly, he explained that his older sister had colic when she was an infant and that today she is a wonderful, sensitive, caring person. And he left. What? That is the light I was waiting for? Not so much being shed if you know what I mean! I need to get out of the house! How? I breast feed every three hours. Who would I leave her with? She screams all the time? I might want to hurt my own child? What? Oh but not to worry! Thirty years from now, she will be a wonderful, sensitive, caring person!

On the way home, Corey couldn't believe it. "I could be a pediatrician!" he shrilly cried. "All you do is walk in, move their little arms and legs, look them over, and say that everything looks great. Did he not notice that she is screaming her head off! That can't be normal! I say that it is pretty convenient for him that none of his patients talk!" He continued to rant and rave about the technological advances of medicine and question the science of pediatrics all the way home. What he really wanted to know was how we were going to make it for three more months. What he was really saying was that there had to be a cure, some drops, a pill, something. What he needed was an answer, a way to solve the problem so that our lives could return to normal. And that is when I first realized it. I had to see it in someone else to recognize it in myself. Corey and I were totally focused on us. We were being selfish and whiny. Not that most people would blame us, and not without reason, but without purpose. Where was it getting us? What was our self-pity helping? Our daughter was in the back seat, miserable, and all we could think about was how overwhelmed we were.

The car ride home from the doctor's office was not just another jaunt from Johnson City to Elizabethton; it was the beginning of a journey back into the arms of my Father. I bowed my head right then and there, with Corey mad at all doctors everywhere and Sophie screaming, and said, "Thank you, dear heavenly Father, for colic." I didn't yet know if I truly meant that statement, but I had to say it. Somewhere down deep, I knew God would get me through this, that God would get all of us through this. You see, for the first time in a long time, I couldn't just fix it! There was no answer, explanation, or cure. It didn't matter if I tried harder, worked harder, or cried harder; nothing was going to change. I could not rely on my own abilities, and I could not control this situation. The only thing left to do was the only thing I should have done in the first place, give it to God. And so as a tired, broken child, I fell into the arms of my Father, and I felt Him catch me. Sophie was not any calmer, nor was Corey for that matter. My storm was not over, but my focus was shifting.

DAY 6

Our search for the answer to the question "What is colic?" had begun. It started with a small flyer that our pediatrician gave us. I had read it several times since we left his office, and I just could not believe what I was reading. The hand out stated, and I quote, "Colic is defined as continual or persistent crying in a baby who is otherwise healthy and well fed, typically lasting between 2-4 hours a day for at least 5 days a week. It usually begins around 2 or 3 weeks of age, and subsides on its own by 12 weeks. It often peaks around 6 weeks. The cause of colic is unknown." Unknown? How can that be? We live in a time when space travel is no longer discussed because putting a man on the moon is old hat. I still have no idea how a fax machine or a cell phone works, but I know someone can explain it to me. We have people undergoing heart transplant surgery daily. You don't have to wear glasses anymore because you can just get your eyes zapped. I can put just about any word imaginable in my Yahoo search and find out anything I want to about that word. I can sit in East Tennessee and IM someone in Japan. BUT the cause of colic is unknown? Does that seem strange to anyone else? Are Corey and I the only people that have ever had a hard time with this? You mean to tell me that for hundreds of years, there have been babies crying non-stop for the first three months of their lives, and then as quickly as it appears, at three months of age, it disappears, and no one finds that odd? Everyone is just supposed to be satisfied with, "The cause of colic is unknown"? Amazing.

On a more positive note, we did learn that the term

colic is derived from the Greek word *calicos* or *colon,* suggesting that the disorder may stem from the gastrointestinal tract. The flyer also gave us a 1-800 number we could call to order a $90 car simulator. Sophie hates the car.

DAY 8

Our search continues. Honestly, after typing the word colic in on the internet and finding 106,452 hits, my part of the search was over. My husband and my mother, however, continued to search for the secret cure for the ailment with no known cause. I had already hit a wall. It didn't take my being biology major to figure out that if they don't know what causes colic, then they sure don't know how to fix it. My husband and mother would not be so easily deterred.

Corey was more than a little frustrated after reading the first 100 hits of my internet search. They all said the same thing - well except for the equestrian sites. Horses get colic, too. Who knew? Basically, site after site would give the definition - excess crying, healthy baby. Then, there would be suggestions for soothing your baby. Each site would conclude by basically stating that you should not be discouraged if you cannot console your infant because you can do nothing to help your baby because NO ONE KNOWS WHAT COLIC IS! My mother was trying another avenue. I like to call her technique the "Ask Everyone You See" approach. Every day, I would get a call, and most conversations were the same. Mom would call. "Ronda, I know you're tired, so I'll talk fast. I ran into _____ at the grocery store today, and I told them about Sophie having "the colic." _____ said that their granddaughter had it, and all they did was _____, and it just went away." The first blank could usually be filled in by substituting any number of my mother's neighbors, church friends, people my mother used to work with, or on occasion, just someone she met in the grocery store line. The suggestion blank could usually be filled in by an assortment of remedies ranging from cat nip tea and special sleeping wedges to massaging the feet and a trip to the chiropractor. That's right - my mother met people in the Food City with cures ranging from colic pills to ace bandages around the abdomen. Some I tried - most I did not.

I do not pass judgment on any mother, anywhere, for trying any thing that <u>does not harm</u> the baby. Colic is hard, and you cannot blame anyone for trying to find a cure. For me, it wasn't about finding a cure. I was slowly beginning to accept the fact that for the next three months, my child would have colic. And for the next three months, my family had to survive. So that is where my search ended - survival.

DAY 11

Corey did find two interesting pieces of information today. There are two schools of thought. First, there are those who believe colic has to do with an immature digestive system, the idea being that the bowel in a colicky baby contracts much slower than it should, the side effect being excess "wind." (In east Tennessee, we just call that gas.) This leads to discomfort and causes the baby to cry. Unfortunately, the more a baby cries the more air the baby takes in, which can exacerbate the problem. The second school states that babies with colic have an immature neurological system. Because of this immaturity, babies cannot properly deal with the enormous amount of stimuli with which they are coming in contact daily. This is why the sound of the dishwasher or the vacuum cleaner is so soothing. These noises drown out all the other stimuli and allow the baby to relax and sleep. Neither idea is accepted completely. However, most pediatricians do believe colic is related to discomfort in the digestive tract.

That's it. That is when the search officially ended. Corey now joined me, and together we had to accept that there was no definite answer and there was no cure. My mother would still continue to call and offer suggestions. She firmly believed that we should take Sophie to a chiropractor. But for Corey and me, it was time to give up the search for answers. We found ourselves hurting for the parents of severely ill children. We didn't know what caused colic, and we didn't know yet how we were going to survive, but we knew our child was healthy, and in three months, this would all be over. We also knew that there were parents out there who knew all the "answers," but knowing didn't change the fact that their child was not healthy and that their child would not be healthy three months from now. We gave up our search with a prayer for those parents. We asked God to send down His peace and His understanding, and we went to bed thanking God that Sophie had colic. And this time we meant it.

DAY 21

I was straightening up some papers around the computer and ran across an article that Corey hadn't shown me. I don't know why it caught my eye really, but I sat down and read it. Within minutes, I knew why Corey had not shown me the article. He knew me well enough to know that I would initially have the urge to find the author and kill him. First of all, it was written by a man. I'm about to sound a little anti-male, but bear with me. I will start by saying that my husband was doing all he could to keep it together. He was trying to work all day, ease my load at night, and honestly trying not to spend every waking moment missing our old life. Because that is what men do? They have to slowly take on this whole parenting thing. They are allowed to ask questions like, "So, should I feed her?" and not look dumb. They are allowed to be a little stand offish and nervous around the baby and not be considered a horrible person. And they are allowed to tell people how they long for pre-parent days, and everyone just laughs. Most daddies take a week off work, and then it's back to life as usual, at least during the day. Corey didn't look any different; I was just starting to wear normal clothes again, really big normal clothes. Corey went out to lunch with his co-workers everyday; I ate whatever food I could find that needed no preparation and could be held in one hand. Corey drove down the road in his car, singing to the radio, calling people on his cell phone; I spent every adventure in the car with a screaming infant in the back (Who, by the way, is not a big fan of the radio or me talking on the phone - more stimuli). My point: no matter how hard we try, the fact is men have a different understanding of their role as parents, and society says that is O.K.

Back to the article, the author was a man, and therefore, I was not going to be very impressed with anything he had to say. I will say, however, it was not the fact that his genetic make-up is XY that was going to get him killed. That was something he was simply born with, a birth defect of sorts, and I could not hold that against him. What incited murderous tendencies within me was what I proceeded to read after the by-line. This doctor, this MALE doctor, described colic as a "powerful rite of passage." His belief being that:

> "Colic exists in order to change deeply ingrained relationship habits. Even after the birth, many parents and families would revert back to their previous schedules and activities if the new baby would only remain quiet and peaceful. It would be easy to continue reading what you like to read, going where you like to go, doing what you like to do as before, if only the baby would ...."

You get the picture. This lunatic was trying to say that "the colic" is the reason I pay attention to my child. That "the colic" is the only thing keeping me from forgetting I gave birth and that I have a daughter. The very idea is absurd! I have never experienced a child without colic, but I am pretty sure that I would remember to hold and care for my child regardless of whether he or she was screaming his or her head off.

I was enraged! Livid! I walked around all day just steamed. How could he say that? Hadn't he read all the other articles out there? The articles that stated over and over again that there was no known cause for colic and that parents in no way should feel guilty because they could not have possibly caused or prevented colic? I could not believe his nerve! I then decided to hate him. Looking back, I'm pretty sure it was just my postpartum talking, but I decided that I could hate him and God would understand. I bet he never had to take care of a colicky baby. I bet he never had to take care of a baby! I bet a man with as little knowledge about women as he has shown isn't even married!! He is an unmarried, never been a father before, never even seen a colicky baby, good for nothing man!!! I called Corey and told him that if he loved me at all, he would hunt down this crazy doctor and beat him up! He reminded me that he liked to consider himself a lover and not a fighter and that he would be home around five. A lot of help he was. Of course, he is a man.

It wasn't until 4:30 AM while holding Sophie, listening to the vacuum, and watching *Harry and the Hendersons* on mute with no close captioning, that my anger started to make sense. He was right. Now wait, don't slam the book shut yet; allow me to explain. The crazy, lunatic, male doctor was right. Do I believe that is why colic exists? No. Do I believe that every child who has colic does so because he or she would have been neglected otherwise? Of course not, but for me, he was right.

I am one of those people who have always said that the more I have to do, the better. I have always filled my days to capacity, running on the adrenalin of having too many irons in the fire. Anyone one knows me knows that I always have several projects going on at once, and I love making enormous check lists at the beginning of the day and marking through each accomplished task. I have even been known to write things down I have already done just so I can mark them off. But colic had changed all that. Pre-colicky baby, I would have told you that once Sophie was born, I was probably going to return to work because I loved being a teacher. I would have explained that even if I did not return to work, I would at least continue to be the cheerleading coach. My husband and I would start our college bible study up again in February as well as a much needed date night. I had already made plans for someone to teach my Sunday school class until the last Sunday in January, but I would be back after that. I envisioned Sophie going to basketball games, youth outings, retreats, shopping, interpretive movement practice, etc. My life wasn't really going to change; I was just adding another project. Becoming a mom just meant a few more tasks on the daily checklist.

Colic changed everything. My life had shut down. There were no meetings, no ball games, no pep-rallies, and certainly no date night. There wasn't even time to make a check list, not that it mattered because there would have been only one entry: take care of colicky baby. Sophie didn't need a mom who had it all together. She didn't need a mom who could juggle work, church, friends, and marriage. Sophie needed a mom who could rock and walk and bounce and hold her all day long. "The colic" had made me that mom.

God knew that I wouldn't go down without a fight. He saw me white knuckling my old, hectic life style. He could see the future, and He knew Sophie was about to become a mark on a checklist. So there I was, on the couch, in my now three day old pajamas/uniform, holding the most precious little girl I had ever seen, and as I watched her sleeping, I realized that a colicky baby was the answer to a prayer I had been praying for years. Over the past few years, my prayer style had changed. I would pray each day for God's will for my life. There were times when I longed to pray more detailed prayers, but the bottom line was He knew what was best for me, so why not just pray for His will and be done. Over the past few years, any time anything positive happened in my life, I would thank God and somehow know that it was because I trusted Him to lead me. When things were going well, it was because I truly had given the control to my heavenly Father. But now, when things weren't so good and I couldn't see beyond the next inconsolable crying spell, I wasn't looking for God's hand at all. And yet, there it was. God spoke loudly and clearly through a crazy, lunatic, male doctor. I needed colic. My family needed colic. The busyness was gone, and the checklists were out the window. Each day consisted of trusting in God for strength and loving a little girl who needed her mom's and dad's undivided attention.

DAY 22

One hint that I actually found helpful was the use of a front carrier. My friend Brianna suggested that the warmth and closeness might help calm Sophie while allowing me a little more freedom. She let me borrow her *Baby Bjorn* carrier, and I loved it! Notice I said I loved it. Sophie liked it and especially enjoyed it if we were out and about. As for helping with the crying - not really. I did however find it very liberating to be able to bounce a baby while dusting. I give the front carrier two thumbs up for mothers of colicky babies everywhere.

Chapter Four
It's All About Me

DAY 26

As we started month two of "the colic," I felt as though I had a better grip on things. The facts were simple. Colic had no known cause and, therefore, no known cure. My husband and I needed to hold on until March 26 (ironically, Corey's birthday) because for no known reason, "the colic" would just disappear. I now realized that my situation could be worse and that I needed to be thankful for my healthy baby girl. I knew that only God could get me through this, and that is where I believed my heart was, with God. So that is how this week started, this month started on track and ready to face a colicky baby. I would not be facing this baby alone, however; all of heaven was coming with me.

By 8:15 AM I was not feeling so inspired. As I have said before, Sophie's day started about 7:00 AM, and 1 hour and 15 minutes later I was ready to throw in the towel. There were those voices in my head, no, not those kinds of voices. The voices in my head said that I must be doing something wrong, the voices that said other mothers are out shopping with their babies right now. O.K., maybe not at 8:15 AM, but they would be shopping soon enough. The voices that said look at you. You can't even make it 2 hours without crying. You are a sad, pathetic little momma. You stay in your pajamas all day, and all you get accomplished is holding a baby who frankly doesn't seem to like you very much. This would continue until Corey would call. Corey would call to check on us, and I would want to make sure he knew how horrible my life was. I would cry, sound depressed, and make sure he truly understood that I was being a martyr. Before he hung up the phone, he needed to comprehend all that I had given up for our daughter, who by the way hated me. Other people would call or stop by, and I made sure that they understood how bad my life was. I needed them to pity me and feel sorry for me. I needed them to give me extra attention and show me as much sympathy as possible. Unfortunately, none of this made me feel any better. This was not me. I mean, don't get me wrong, I liked to complain, but it was usually for comic relief. Or maybe, this was me. Could this be me? Is this the person I truly was? Was I the woman who told everyone to rely on God for strength and guidance, but really I just fixed things myself or told everybody and their brother about my situation until things got better? I had now spent the first weeks of my daughter's life worrying about me. I had spent day after day wondering how I would get through. But could it be that I had spent 28 years only thinking of me? Was I actually one of those annoying, self-absorbed, obnoxious people that think the world revolves around them?

I didn't have the time or the energy to shave my legs. Therefore, I surely did not have the time or the energy to ponder life changing questions about the very fiber of my being. I dismissed these notions and went back to the monotony of caring for a crying baby. But the seed had been planted, and somehow I knew God wasn't through with this conversation just because I thought I was.

DAY 27

They say just about everything can be blamed on your mother, so that is where I started. You see, I was right. God wasn't going to let this one just slide by. For the next three days, all I could think about was, "Am I that person? Am I that self-absorbed, annoying, obnoxious, selfish person?" And I was wrong about not having the time or the energy. What else did I have to do while Sophie slept? If you'll remember, as a side effect of colic, Sophie was an extremely light sleeper. If she finally fell asleep, the worst thing you could do was attempt to lay her down. You would very quickly find yourself back at square one. So who was I kidding? I was sitting at the end of our couch, muscle cramp in the arm, afraid to move, listening to a vacuum cleaner for at least an hour a day. So what else did I have to do? God had trapped me. I had kept myself so busy for so long that it had been years since I had taken a really hard look at myself. Now faced with the inevitable, I did the only thing I could do; I blamed someone else.

I spent the day explaining to God that I really couldn't help the way I had turned out. It was very simple really; it was my mother's fault. That's right; I was now a mother and still felt no qualms about turning on my own. I would like to say in her defense that she had the best intentions in the world. My mother longed for my life to be perfect. In an effort to make my life perfect, she devoted every minute of every day to insuring my complete happiness. Every dollar, every weekend, every ounce of energy her little 5 ft. frame could muster up was given freely to my brother and me. You see, I grew up in a home where it was all about me - all about my wants, my needs, my interests, my plans, my hopes, and my dreams. There was no time for my mother to have any semblance of a life of her own because it was all about me. There was no money for her to have anything nice because it was all about me. And there was definitely no energy left at the end of the day because it was all about me. All her co-workers knew all about me. All her friends in many ways became my friends because they knew all about me. She had devoted her whole life to me. And what had I done to repay her generosity? What had I done to show her how much I appreciated her love and support? I had become selfish. I had become the kind of daughter that gave too little and said thank you not nearly often enough. How could I have not seen it before? My mom had given her life up for me, and I took off and never looked back. And you know what? She never expected me to. My mother loved me with an unconditional love, and I was spending my days loving Sophie conditionally. Did she sleep? Yes. Oh, how mommy loves you! Did she cry all morning? Yes. Oh, how frustrated is mommy? Did I have time for myself today? No. What have I done to my life?

"Am I that person? Am I that woman?" The answer was becoming more and more clear. God was speaking at almost audible level now, but I still wasn't convinced. I couldn't possibly be that person. Not me!

DAY 29

The next morning, I felt this overwhelming feeling of "this is not about your mother - this is about you." God woke me up with this gnawing thought running through my head over and over as if it was my new mantra, only I didn't choose it. "This is not about your mother - this is about you." I couldn't shake it; believe me, I tried. "This is not about your mother - this is about you." I hated the way I was feeling. I had too much on me. Too little sleep and too much crying in my life and I was finally cracking up. And that is when it hit me. Why hadn't I seen it before? It wasn't my mother's fault; it was my mother's and my husband's fault. Yes, yes that's it! I was a pawn in a game of someone else's choosing. The world was lucky I turned out as selfless as I did. I started out in a home that was all about me and quickly became part of a marriage that was all about me. Well, there you go. When in doubt, blame everything on your mother, and if that doesn't work move on to the husband.

Since Corey and I met, he had devoted himself to me and my happiness. I wish I was exaggerating. Elaborate gifts, Saturdays devoted to me (not the golf course or the softball field), requesting permission to do anything other than spend time with me, and playing with my hair every night until I fell asleep. Now, I know what some of you are thinking, "I like a man with some backbone, not just a push over!" Trust me - Corey's no push over. O.K., maybe just a little, but trust me - life is not bad. He made every day all about me. My mother made every day all about me. I was trapped! It's not my fault. What was a woman to do?

God had an answer. He knew what "a woman" was

to do. God was opening my eyes, and what I was seeing wasn't pretty. My life was all about take, take, take. For 28 years, take, take, take. "The colic" didn't care about what kind of life I had become accustomed to. God was tired of the kind of life I had become accustomed to. And honestly, I was sickened by the kind of life I had become accustomed to. It had been all about me for far too long. I asked God for forgiveness and for the first time sat peacefully and watched my baby sleep. I wasn't worried about the fact that I hadn't showered or brushed my teeth. I wasn't consumed with how my wishes and wants for the day had been thrown out the window. I was content just holding her. I was content just meeting her needs. I was Sophie's biological mother because I got pregnant and gave birth. I would become Sophie's mommy when I came to realize that her needs were more important than my own. I would become a better person when I began to live as though it was not all about me. Because you know what? It's not.

DAYS 30-35

I spent the next several days working through all of this. I took a really hard look at myself and realized I needed to change my thoughts on motherhood. There had to be a balance. Being a mother wasn't about giving up every hope and dream I ever had for myself. Being a mother wasn't about losing my identity to my child. And being a mother certainly wasn't about putting my child first and my husband second. On the other hand, I had only been a mother for a few weeks, but I could already tell being a mother would be about sacrifice. I felt as though I had been lied to for years. All I ever heard was that I could do it all. I truly believed I could do it all. But now, locked up in my house, forced to reevaluate my life, I realized I couldn't do it all. I couldn't be an amazing teacher, mother of the year, and a wonderful wife. Something would suffer. I could see my future. I would want to be a good teacher because besides loving it, I was getting paid to do so. I would probably feel so guilty at the end of the day for not having been with Sophie that discipline and the word "no" would probably be out the window. I wouldn't want to spend my only moments a day with her fussing at her. I would spend all evening giving her all my attention, and when she went to bed, I would soon follow. I suddenly realized that there was no Corey in this equation. There was no date night, no cuddling on the couch, and definitely no lingerie. Society had told me that I could do it all, but society was wrong. In an attempt to do it all, my marriage would suffer. And although Corey and I had thrown around the idea of me not going back to work, the answer was now very clear. I loved teaching, I loved my students, and I am still paying back student loans from my

Master's degree, but there was a sacrifice that needed to be made. My role had to change. It wasn't just about me anymore. It should have been more about Corey all along, but it took a demanding little girl for me to finally see it. I would no longer be Ronda Paulson Science teacher. I would need to become Ronda Paulson wife and mother.

DAY 36

It was Valentine's Day, and Corey and I were scheduled to attend a Song of Solomon conference with breast pump Brianna and her husband Bill. My mother had graciously offered to give up her romantic evening to keep Sophie. I say graciously because Sophie was not an easy child to baby sit. My mother came over, and after taking several pictures of Sophie in her "Be Mine" bib, hat, and matching socks, Corey and I were free at last. We couldn't believe it. We were going out to eat and out for the evening with friends. We spent the entire night laughing, flirting, and listening to a minister talk about sex. That's right, sex. If you haven't ever read "Song of Solomon," you are missing out. Well honestly, you will probably need an interpreter as we did because at first glance, there isn't too much sexy about a man likening your neck to the tower of David and your hair to a flock of goats. By the time we left, Bill and my husband were making jokes about going to the "garden."

We arrived home, and my mother met us at the door. Suddenly, the reality of our situation hit us like a wall. My mother looked rattled, to say the least. A friend of hers had come over to help, and she was out the door and in the car before I even said, "Hi."

"How was it?" I asked.

"Awful. Awful. I mean awful." My mother just mumbled these words as she collected her things. Sophie had been her usual self, loud and inconsolable. "I just can't take it, Ronda! She just cries and cries and cries. Your life is hell, isn't it?" With that question still hanging in the air, we both began to laugh. I hugged mom and apologized. I think she was crying when she left. I felt so bad for putting her through such a rough evening.

Corey finally got our little one to sleep and came to bed. When he got there, he found his wife in a little red number she had picked up for Valentine's Day. We held each other and kissed, and it was nice. I won't give out any more details except to say that Corey was just about to the "garden" when Sophie began to cry. Her timing was impeccable. How did she know? Corey looked at me, and I looked at him. Both of us were wondering the same thing, would she go back to sleep? The next round of cries was louder, and that gave us our answer. We both began to laugh, hard. We laughed all the way to the den to pick her up. We smiled at each other across the couch as we took turns holding her. There was a time that this would have devastated us. We would have been mad at Sophie and mad at the world. Slowly, we were coming to realize that it wasn't all about us anymore. There would be times when our needs would come first. There would be romantic evenings and trips to the garden in the future. But for right now, Sophie had to come first, and that was O.K.

The next morning, Bill asked Corey if he made it to the "garden." Corey and I just looked at each other, and then Corey answered, "The gate keeper wouldn't let me in." We all laughed at the reality of being parents and at the joy of being parents. And for once, I'm not being sarcastic.

DAYS 37-50

The rest of the month was more of the same. Sophie did not seem to be getting any better, but she definitely wasn't getting any worse. There were good days and bad days. On the good, I freely let God take over. On the bad, there were times when I just didn't know what to pray. And that is when I learned a very valuable lesson. Prayer isn't always spoken. Sometimes, my prayer was holding Sophie and feeling the miraculous nature of God in my arms. Sometimes, my prayer was a hot shower and the feeling of rejuvenation that came with it. Sometimes, my prayer was an overwhelming feeling of thankfulness for my daughter and my husband. Sometimes, I wouldn't have the strength to pray, and for the first time in my life, I would openly ask the Holy Spirit to intercede for me. Sometimes, my prayer was a song, and sometimes, my prayer was one word, "Help." But most often, my prayer was simply, "Please Dear Heavenly Father, calm my anxious heart." It was my way of giving over power each day. I needed God to be in control of my out-of-control life, and the best way for me to hand over the reins was to simply say, "Calm my anxious heart." And you know what? He would. Without fail and often without hesitation, God would calm my heart and take over. It was the only way I was going to make it. Because if you'll remember, "the colic" wasn't over, we still had one month to go!

Chapter Five
There Is A Light

DAY 53

And, the countdown begins. Twenty-three days and "the colic" is supposed to magically disappear. I keep trying to remind myself that there is no guarantee that on March 26, 2003, Sophie will be colic free. The articles always say "around twelve weeks" the symptoms of colic seem to ease. I keep trying not to get my hopes up because "around twelve weeks" is a pretty vague point of reference. I am trying to prepare myself for what I will do if Sophie isn't colic free in twenty-three days. Regardless, my mind and my husband are chanting, "No more colic in twenty-three days!"

But then what? I mean, I'm finding it a little hard to believe that one day, voila, no more colic. Somewhere in the dark recesses of my mind, I see Sophie in a dorm room, falling asleep to the sound of a vacuum cleaner - O.K., maybe just a sound machine. I see her screaming in the bath tub for the next 12-15 years. I see Corey and me maintaining our now customary routine of meeting at the door and passing off the kid from now until she is too big to pass off. Considering my husband's and my size and stature, we are probably talking at least another sixteen years. The television will continue to stay on mute, and all of our friends will have given up on us. They'll say things behind our backs like, "Do you remember how much fun we used to have with Corey and Ronda? It's so sad really, Sophie having colic for going on five years and all." I've now lost 42 pounds and so, if my calculations are correct, I will weigh in the negatives by this time next year. Corey will have finally given up all hope of ever having sex again, and cat hair will have over taken our house. This is what life with Sophie is like, and this is all I know. What will the next twenty-three days bring? Only time will tell.

DAY 56

Hallelujah! There is a light! I have seen the light! There is a light at the end of the colic tunnel! You are not going to believe the day I had. Sophie took a nap. Sophie slept, in her bassinet, for two whole hours. I cleaned my house! I dusted, cleaned the bathroom, and ran the sweeper. I mean, the vacuum was already going, so why not put it to good use! I cannot believe how good it felt to clean my house. I loved every minute of it. I felt like a real person. But that's not all. Sophie also slept in her bassinet from 8:00-11:00 PM. And while I will keep many details to myself, let me just say, the long awaited trip to "the garden" was worth the wait! That's right! I cleaned my house and had sex! I am a real person! I feel so alive and rejuvenated. Thank you Lord for lemon scented Pledge and sex. Who knew that is all it would take? Two naps in her bassinet, and Sophie has a new mom. I feel as though I can face anything "the colic" wants to throw at me. All this time, I have been praying for strength and endurance. I have been seeking guidance and reassurance. I have asked God to give me what I would need to make it through this ordeal, and today, God answered - not in the way I thought He would, but He answered. God sent lemon scented Pledge and an uninterrupted trip to "the garden." I really feel like I can make it now. Twenty days, thirty days, forty.... well, let's not get carried away, but I can make it. Corey, Sophie, and I are going to make it.

And do you now what is waiting on the other side of colic? Normalcy, the normalcy that I have taken for granted for far too long. The normalcy of just being with my husband. The normalcy of playing with my daughter. The normalcy of being a stay at home mom. I'm beginning to understand something about myself. If I had had that kind of normalcy from day one, I would have taken life with Sophie for granted and returned to the every day business of being me. But now, I long for the hum drum. I long for the mundane. At this point in my life, this colic-driven point in my life, I take nothing for granted. Every experience is better than I remember it being in my pre-colic life. A hot shower is a gift from God. Cleaning my house, which was drudgery before, now gives me a new outlook on life. There is a light! Thank You, Dear Heavenly Father, for Your omniscience. Thank You for helping me see life through new eyes. Thank You for Your blessings, and please help me not to take the simple pleasures of this life for granted.

DAY 61

I will never forget today, for as long as I live. Other mothers fill their baby books with trivial "firsts," such as baby's first smile, baby's first coo, and baby's first laugh. Fluff, mere fluff. Not that I am bitter. No, no, not me. I don't mind that up until now I have had nothing to enter on the "Baby's First Year" calendar except crying. I'm not kidding. December entry: Took first bath; hated it. January entry, under special moments: You cried all month, but we decided to love you anyway. February entry: Took first trip to Target; you hated it. But now for my March entry, it will read: Took first bath without screaming as though someone were killing you! That's right; Sophie took a bath today without crying. I honestly can't believe it. After 8 ½ weeks of taking a bath every other day, after a total of 25 baths in her lifetime, she didn't cry. She just lay there looking at me. Pleasantly would be a stretch, but she just lay there. And afterwards, when we would normally have had World War III over putting on lotion and clothes, she just lay there. No tears, no red face from screaming, just a sweet little baby laying on a towel letting her mother dry her off and take care of her. She will never know how much mom needed that little thank you, but God did. You see, there are a couple of babies at my church that are about the same age as Sophie. It has been so hard to listen to other mothers talk about their babies smiling and cooing. As a matter of fact, Corey and I as a defense mechanism would decide on the drive home from church that they were lying. That's right - they were lying and making up stories right in the middle of the church nursery. Have they no shame? Down deep, though, I knew. I knew other babies smiled and seemed happy, and it killed me that Sophie did not. I longed for just a glimpse of pleasure. Not even as much for myself anymore. I longed to know that she wasn't miserable. And today, God said, "Ronda, your baby isn't miserable." Oh, there is a light, and it is getting brighter and brighter everyday!

DAY 62

My in-laws came to town today. Sophie was taking her first nap EVER in her crib when they arrived, so we ate lunch and visited until she woke up. After she awoke from her nap, she ate, Mary Jane loved on her, and then I took her back upstairs for another nap. Now, keep in mind this is all new to me. Sophie has sporadically started napping during the day over the past two weeks, but this day has been by far her best day ever. I mean, I am in shock. I am truly in a state of awe as I walk down stairs. As I sat down in my living room, still in a daze over the potential of this new life of which I was beginning to see a glimpse, my father-in -law quickly brought me back to reality.

Allow me to preface this next story by saying I love my father-in-law. His name is Carmen, and although he is a little quirky, I love him - I truly do. Also, for the record, I am not just saying that because I know he will read this - I truly love the man. With that being said, I almost killed my father-in-law today. That's right. I almost murdered Carmen with my bare hands. As I sat down in the living room, Carmen looked at me and said, "Well, I don't see what the big deal is. She seems fine to me. I mean, look at all the free time you have while she naps." You see, at this point, Carmen and Mary Jane were still living in Indiana, and all they knew of "the colic" was what we would tell them over the phone. That being said, I still almost killed him. I could feel anger creeping up the back of my neck. I didn't know how to respond. I had just lived two of the hardest months of my life. How could I possibly sum it up in a sentence that would make him understand? As my mind was racing and my face was beginning to redden, my mother-in-law answered for me. "Carmen, it hasn't been like this. Sophie is just now starting to nap." Carmen's answer, "Oh." And the conversation moved on. And that was it.

As for my anger and my need to make him understand, gone. That is definitely one of the many lessons colic has taught me. It doesn't matter if non-colic parents think you are exaggerating, stressing over nothing, or wimping out because your child is a little fussy. It doesn't matter if every time someone comes over to help you, your child is better than he or she has ever been and that person leaves thinking you are causing your child to be colicky because you are too anxious. And it definitely doesn't matter if your father-in-law ever understands. Colic is real, and colic is hard. But just like life, the only person who needs to understand is God, and He does. He is with you every night as you hold your crying little angel. He is with you every morning when you think, "Can I do this again today?" And He is with you when you just don't think you can take it anymore. And at that moment, He sends a light, His light.

DAYS 65-75

I do not want to lead anyone astray. The last two weeks of March were not necessarily colic free. They were however, much improved. You could tell the colic was fading, and it made the days seem easier. She was still quite fussy at times, especially from about 5:00 PM-9:00 PM. At this point however, 5-9 seemed very doable. My family did not always agree. Corey and I were taking a parenting class on Tuesday nights and therefore needed a babysitter from about 5:30-8:00 each week. We decided so as not to dump the colic load on any one person, we would alternate grandparents. I will have to say, each grandmother had her own way of dealing with the colic. Corey's mom, Nana, would greet us at the door, take Sophie who often times would be screaming, and wave good-bye as she said, "Have a good time and don't worry about a thing. We will be fine. Now go on and don't worry." Upon our return, we would enter the house to hear Sophie screaming and to find Mary Jane still smiling. We would ask how the evening went, and she would always answer, "She was fine. I don't mind taking care of her at all." Mary Jane seemed to always remain calm and lie.

Then there was my mother, Mimi. Mimi would arrive at our house and hesitantly enter saying, "How is she doing today?" As we left she would be saying, "Hurry home! Your daughter needs you!" I specifically remember one evening when Corey and I forgot to take the cell phone inside with us. When we got to the car we found four missed calls from my mother. I was scared to death and frantically called home. My brother answered the phone.

"Ryan, what's wrong?" I asked.

Ryan simply answered, "Come home now."

"Why what's wrong?"

"Ronda, she's been screaming all night!"

"Ryan, she has colic; that is what she does!"

I arrived home to find my mom, my dad, and my brother waiting on the porch. Come to find out they had called all over Johnson City to try to find us because they were going to bring Sophie to us. That's right. These three sane individuals had decided that Sophie needed me, so they were going to bring her to me or make me come home. My brother left swearing off children. My father left shaking his head. And Mimi, well Mimi left crying because in her own words, "I just can't take it when she cries!" I yelled after them as they pulled away "Couldn't you just lie like Mary Jane?" As I said, *Corey and I* had learned to handle things pretty well at this point, and overall, things were getting better.

DAY 76

We hit a low today. This was it, our three month mark. The date that we had told ourselves over and over again meant nothing but yet meant everything. It was Corey's 29th birthday, and I thought Sophie and I had an understanding that the perfect gift would be no more colic. Sophie obviously was confused. She spent most of the afternoon crying, and Corey and I both hit a wall. Corey was frustrated, and I felt sorry for him and Sophie and on this day, mostly myself. We came home after a family get together tired and angry. I came in and checked our answering machine and heard a message from a friend who had a son the same age as Sophie. I am awful at returning messages, but for some reason I immediately picked up the phone and called her back. Come to find out, her son also had colic. She had spent the past three months dealing with the same feelings and emotions I had. We talked for an hour. Words cannot express how good it felt to know that she understood. She had no answers, no magic cure, and no suggestions. We just talked. God had been there for me every step of the way. I had seen Him use many different tactics to assure me of His presence. And today, today God used a phone call from a mother of a colicky baby to comfort me like never before.

When I got off the phone, I told Corey that our friend and her husband were going to take their son to a chiropractor. Although we do not condemn their decision or even think bad of it, Corey and I decided to give it another week. It was a rough evening, but we realized that "around three months" meant just that, "around three months." Tomorrow would be another day, and together with God we would face whatever the colic would throw at us, but we would face it tomorrow.

April 4

DAY 85

We are colic free! Sophie takes two naps a day. She sleeps from 9:00 AM-11:00 AM and then goes back down around 1:30 PM and sleeps till around 4:00 PM. She still has a tendency to be fussy in the evening, but I hear that is very common even with non-colicky babies. She goes to bed at 7:30 PM and sleeps until 7:30 AM. She takes baths and actually enjoys them. She does not mind the car anymore and loves her stroller. She cries if she is tired or hungry, and Corey and I both can accept that. There is a light, and it is here! We are at the end of the colic tunnel, and life colic-free is a beautiful, beautiful thing! A friend of mine, who is from Brazil, was trying to quote a very famous saying to Corey and me on this most important day when in her authentic Brazilian accent she said, "That which does not kill us...., Oh yes, that which does not kill us, will make us sick!" Corey and I began to laugh hard! She had just summed up what seemed to have been the past three months of our lives. In the midst of the throws of colic, we did not feel as though we were getting stronger; we just felt sick. We had no idea how God would use Sophie's colic, and we definitely didn't feel stronger. We just felt relieved that is was over.

We were wrong though - we were stronger. We were stronger, and over the next few months, we would see the wonderful work of the Potter's hand. We were merely clay, and God had been molding us for the past three months. It was not pleasant, it did not feel good, and we were glad it was over, but we would soon see the beauty of God's new creation. That which does not kill us will make us sick, then stronger.

Chapter Six
Where Is Sophie Now?

April 5-present day

Where is Sophie now? She is living life colic free and happy. I remember so vividly thinking my child will never be normal. My life will never be normal. I remember believing with all my heart that colic was permanent and that all the articles that said it would go away "around twelve weeks" were lying. Why would there be a colic conspiracy? Simple. Doctors knew they had to lie to mothers because if they told them the truth (that colic is permanent), they would refuse to take their babies home. Mothers would begin striking and refusing to leave the waiting room until someone cured their children. Pediatricians' offices everywhere would be taken over by crazed, sleep-deprived mothers and their colicky babies. Other children would not be able to get the help they needed, offices would close, and the health care system as we know it would crumble. So, the lie is perpetuated to save children everywhere.

But I was wrong. I know that if you are currently dealing with a colicky baby, the above stated scenario seems very feasible to you, but I promise colic does go away, and miraculously your child returns to normal. Sophie sleeps, eats, plays, crawls, smiles and yes, she even laughs. She loves hugs and kisses and singing. She chases our cat and growls at our dog. She is fascinated by other children and Baby Einstein videos. Most of our days are as follows:

7:45 AM	wake, change diaper, and eat breakfast
8:15	play in playpen while Mom and Dad eat breakfast
8:45	change diaper after morning "shoo-shoo"
9:00	watch video

9:45	morning nap
11:30	wake, change diaper, run errands (She loves Wal-Mart.)
12:15 PM	lunch
12:30	play with Mommy, take a walk, visit neighbors
2:00	afternoon nap
4:30	wake, change diaper, eat dinner
5:00	Daddy comes home play with Mommy and Daddy, go out to eat, etc.
8:00	night time bottle
8:15 PM	bed
8:30	Mommy and Daddy time!

I include this schedule only to reiterate the fact that your child and your life will again be normal.

Are there any lingering side effects from "the colic"? I don't think it would be a fair assessment to say that there are colic side effects, but there are some behavioral modifications because of the way I handled "the colic." Allow me to explain. Because Sophie cried all the time, we never really went anywhere. Because we never really went anywhere, I never gave her a bottle. Because I never gave her a bottle, she hated the bottle when I tried to introduce it at 3 ½ months. Note to self: introduce bottle earlier and let Dad share in the feeding of the baby. Secondly, Sophie is very clingy. It is getting better all the time, but she still really likes her Mommy. I attributed that to the fact that I never left her. I did not want to burden my mother-in-law because she is my mother-in-law, and you hate to abuse those who are not blood. I DID want to burden my mother, but it was too hard because she always left crying (my mother, not Sophie). I did not dare leave her with a baby sitter because I was afraid they might become frustrated with her and injure her in some way. I did leave her in the church nursery every Sunday, but without fail, I would always be called out and would spend half of the service attempting to calm my child. So basically for 3 ½ months, it was just Sophie and me. After the colic, Sophie did begin spending more and more time with her grandparents, and Corey and I even went on a five day vacation to Naples, FL. But, between "the colic" and my being a stay at home mom, Sophie still likes us to be together as much as possible.

Sophie is not a bubbly child. She is easily scared and is somewhat apprehensive of strangers, but that is who she is. None of these characteristics do I attribute to colic, but "the colic" did teach me to love her exactly the way she is. Sophie is very attentive and alert. She investigates everything and everybody. My father says she can stare you down like nobody's business, and my neighbor always says, "That ain't no monkey-see, monkey-do baby!" She is strong willed and does things in her own time, and I am beginning to appreciate that about her. Sophie very seldom cries, and when she does, it is usually associated with a very tired little girl or a new tooth. She claps her hands, sings, and dances. She smiles from ear to ear when she sees familiar faces, drinks from a sippie cup, and pulls up on everything. She brings so much joy to my life every day, and I do not know what I ever did without her.

I present all of this not to brag about my daughter but to give hope. I really thought these days would never come. Yet, here I am, loving my daughter, loving life, and having enough free time to write a book. This information is simply part of my closing argument. Colic is real, colic is hard, but colic is survivable.

From one Colic Mommy to another, I will end with this: my favorite part of the day now is going to get my daughter in the morning. I listen to her breathing on the monitor and smile. I hear her flip over, and I get a little excited about the thought of another day together. I strain to hear her "coo" and "ah" and then begin my ascent up the stairs. As I reach her door, I hear her rustle the covers in an attempt to stand, and as I peek through the crack in the door, I see her straining to find me. I slowly open the door asking, "Where is my baby?" As I round the doorway and our faces finally meet, we both begin to smile and laugh. She begins to bounce with excitement, and in my head, I hear her saying, "Get me, Momma, get me!" As I lift her out of her crib, she hugs my neck and we embrace for a moment before we begin our day. As I undress her to change her diaper, she laughs as I kiss and say good morning to each little body part. I hug her again as I pick her up from the changing table, and we go downstairs for breakfast. I finally have my normalcy. I finally have my hum drum. The day I thought would never come is now my reality. Colic is bad, but God is good.

Chapter Seven
Why God
Made Colic

Why God Made Colic

The answer to the question "Why did God make colic?" has three parts. Therefore, in order to completely answer the question, I must do so in sections. The first section answers why God gave Sophie colic. Lessons 1-8 are all valuable lessons that I may have never learned any other way. Lesson 9 is the result of a lot of soul searching. This lesson reveals why I believe God made colic as well as other struggles we may have to endure while on this earth. And lastly, lesson 10 answers the question, "What do I do?" In lesson 10, I share what God has shown me about how to deal with difficult situations.

Lesson One
Everyone Has His or Her Own Test to Pass

My friend Brianna always brings this story up whenever we reminisce about Sophie's colic adventure. She recalls a phone conversation we had upon finding out an acquaintance of ours had recently had a miscarriage. Brianna, who endured two miscarriages before the birth of her daughter, was talking about how much she hurt for this person. We then began to discuss why bad things happen to good people. It was during this part of our conversation that I made the following statement: "If God will not give you more than you can handle, then He must think I am a pretty weak person. I mean honestly, I just don't think my faith has ever been tested. I'm pretty sure He realizes that if I ever have more on my plate than a bad hair day, I am going to crumble." Brianna still laughs as she insinuates that I practically asked God for a colicky baby. I must admit I laugh too, now. I laugh because although colic is not life threatening and although many parents and children go through much worse everyday, everyone has his or her own test to pass. God gave me colic. For those who have not lived it, they probably see it as no worse than a bad hair day. But the bottom line is, this is not a competition. As Christians, we do not have to have the most amazing turn around testimony story ever. We do not have to have horrible things happen to us by the world's standards. And we do not have to prove our holiness by telling everyone we see how hard our lives are. We do however have a test to pass. This life is a test, a preparation ground for the life to come, and we need to take it one day at a time. We need to pass each test, regardless of how big or how small, and give God all the glory when we receive our passing grade. Thank You, God, for seeing my family through a very difficult time. Thank You for making what could have been just an unpleasant experience a time of growth and understanding. Thank You for helping me pass my test. I pray that You will begin strengthening me now for whatever else the future holds. Give us all the strength not to ask why but to instead hit our knees and ask for help.

Lesson Two
God Is Always Just a Prayer Away

The reason I titled this book <u>Why God Made Colic-A First Time Mother's Journey</u> is because that is what it has been, a journey. Before the birth of my daughter, I considered myself a strong Christian and believed that I tried to live each day for Christ. Yet looking back, I spent the first month of my child's life giving little to no attention to God. I wasn't praying, I wasn't reading my Bible, I wasn't meditating, I was just trying to survive on my own. That, however, is not the surprising part. The surprising part is this: God was still just a prayer away. He had not left me in my time of need. He had not forsaken me during this very difficult period. He was in the exact place He had always been, eagerly waiting for me. And even though I had left Him, there He was with open arms. He had been waiting in the wings, hurting for me, longing for me, and as soon as I asked, He was there. Now don't get me wrong. Unlike many of my prayers, God did not rush in and immediately eradicate the colic problem. But He was there. I could feel His presence. I could feel His peace. He was where He is still to this day, just a prayer away.

Lesson Three
Even When You Don't Know What to Ask- You Shall Receive

I have spent my whole life as a member of the Christian church. I have attended countless Sunday school classes, retreats, bible schools, and church camps. I have memorized scripture and sung more praise songs than I ever thought possible to learn. However, throughout the years, there has been one very important concept about which I have been taught very little. The Holy Spirit. Very few lessons ever center on the Holy Spirit. Very few songs and retreat topics are based on the Holy Spirit. Now, don't get me wrong. Over the years, I have been taught about the Trinity, but even during those times, the Holy Spirit was never really explained to me. Who would have guessed that "the colic" would teach me about the Holy Spirit? Well, besides God.

I remember sitting in my living room, holding a crying baby, not knowing what to do, unable to think clearly, and unable to even ask for help. I felt lost, confused, angry, and sleep deprived. And at that moment, I learned a very valuable lesson about the Holy Spirit. I closed my eyes and said out loud, "Holy Spirit, please pray for me because I do not know what to pray!" I repeated that prayer several times, and I firmly believe the Holy Spirit interceded for me. I did not even know what I needed at that moment in time. Words were of no use because I was so confused. My emotions were heightened, and I felt very alone. But I wasn't. The Holy Spirit spoke for me, and a warm rush of peace fell upon me.

God sent His Spirit so that we would never be alone. God sent His Spirit to abide within us until the day of His return. And God sent His Spirit so that even when we don't know what to ask- we shall receive.

Lesson Four
God Is Your Audience

I have always put too much stock in what others think. It is truly embarrassing how much time and effort I have wasted over the years wondering what others were thinking. Do they like my hair? Is my outfit O.K.? Can they tell I've gained weight? Can they tell I've lost weight? Am I good enough? Am I funny? Do they know I am trying my best? Are they mad at me? Question after question, year after year, just hoping to please those around me. I could only imagine how my problem would be exacerbated as a mother. Once my daughter was born, I would not only worry about what people thought of me as a Christian, a wife, a teacher, I would now have to worry about what they thought of me as a mother!

Well, let me just say, "the colic" fixed many of my worries for me. Did they think I was a good mother? Probably not. I was probably seen as over dramatic, stressed, and incapable of taking care of a newborn. Did they think Sophie was being properly cared for? Probably not. My child screamed all day long, every day. Did they understand my life at all? Probably not. But for the first time in my life, I did not care.

Who was with me day after day? God. Who heard my cries of frustration? God. Who saw me try and try and try to help my daughter be more comfortable? God. And that is when it hit me. God is my audience. He watches my every move and knows the emotions of my heart. He sees every tear and every smile. God is my audience not "they." God is my audience, and do you know what is most amazing? He likes what He sees.

Lesson Five
I'm Not God

My husband and I have made a lot of jokes lately, most of which have started with, "You know, if I were God...." For example, I might say, "You know, if I were God, I think I would allow men the wonderful, natural experience of breast feeding!" A common example Corey might give would sound something like, "You know, if I were God, I would make a baby that did not fight sleep. I mean it makes no sense and it is very frustrating. I say if you are tired, you should just go to sleep!" Back and forth we would banter, "If I were God, there would be no stretch marks." "If I were God, babies would love to ride in a golf cart." "If I were God, hemorrhoids would just magically disappear." Sometimes the conversation would take a more serious turn, and sometimes it was a way to voice our frustrations. We would imagine that if we were God, there would be no colic, there would be no babies born with birth defects, there would be no horrible stories of how an infant died in her sleep, and there would definitely be no baby or child anywhere going to bed hungry or unloved.

But here's the realization: I'm not God. I can't see the future, and I don't always understand how the past brought me to where I am today. I can choose to not think about hurting children, but God watches over them each and every night and hurts as they hurt. I cannot possibly understand how hard it is to care for a disabled child, but God does. He sits with those parents day in and day out. He washes those children and feeds those children and comforts those children. And I cannot comprehend the loss of a child, but God can. Not only did His son die, He watched as his son cried out, "My God, My God, why have you forsaken me?" I am not God, and I am thankful that I am not. Mostly though, I am thankful for a God that understands my pain and feels my hurt. Thank You, Heavenly Father, for being a God of compassion and love. Thank You for being a God who loves innocent little children as well as a sinner like me.

Lesson Six
Quantity Does Not Equal Quality

My husband's idea of good food is a lot of food. He loves buffets of any kind. The more the better is his motto. Corey cares nothing about food quality. In fact, he hates food that looks as though it is being presented. In his mind, real men do not eat "fru-fru" food unless it is an appetizer or being served with a big slab of beef because to Corey, quantity equals quality.

I think before Sophie I felt the same way, not about food but about serving, about giving of my time. In my mind, the more I was doing, the better Christian I could be. I convinced myself that busyness equaled greatness. I believed that quantity equaled quality. Colic helped me see the light. Because Sophie was so colicky, my life came to a screeching halt. For three months, I was locked in my house with a fussy baby and a vacuum cleaner. After a few weeks of adjusting to sleep depravation, my mind cleared, and I did nothing but think. It was in the slowing down that I learned some very hard but important things about myself. I liked being busy because it made me feel important and needed. Yet now, sitting in my pajamas all day and never leaving the house, I was more needed than ever. I liked being busy because people would applaud my busyness. Now, with the applause gone, I began to realize that the praise of man is no reason to serve. I liked being busy because I did not have to think. Now, with nothing on my hands but time, I saw myself very clearly, and the picture was not pretty. I had been running from service project to youth outing to FCA, and very seldom did I even stop and think about what God wanted from me. I was so busy I did not have time! And suddenly, the irony hit me like a ton of bricks. I was so busy, giving of my time; I was actually being selfish with my time. God wanted my time, and I was too busy to give it to Him.

God is now showing me that it is not busyness that makes you a servant. It is not the approval or the cheers of those around you. And it is not about needing to feel important. Serving is not only in big projects and productions. Serving is often in the quiet moments when there is no one there to notice. I am learning more and more each day about what it means to be a true servant for God. It is truly amazing how often I keep messing up, but I will keep trying. And each day, I will continue to remind myself that busyness does not equal greatness anymore than quantity equals quality.

Lesson Seven
Changing a Diaper Is Worship

I was totally convinced that at the time I needed God most, I did not have time for Him. The reason being, when you are in the throws of colic, you do not have time for a "quiet time." Don't get me wrong. You long for any quiet time at all, but you just do not have time to sit down and read the Bible. My pediatrician recommended not going to the church nursery for about 4-6 weeks, and needless to say, Sophie was not content to sit through a church service on my lap. We had temporarily and indefinitely cancelled our small group bible study, and because I wasn't going to church, I was not teaching Sunday school. Therefore, I concluded that if I had no time for bible study, no time for fellowship, no time for teaching, and no time for a church service, I had no time for God. How could I have been so confused for so long? Had I really spent the last 28 years believing that God was only around when I was participating in church activities or personal bible study?

The answers to these questions came as God reached out to me. He showed me over the next few months that He was always there and that worship was giving Him praise, period. Worship wasn't just singing the words projected on a screen. Worship wasn't just going to church or teaching Sunday school. Worship is giving praise and glory to God wherever you are and through whatever you are doing. I soon learned that I could worship God while feeding Sophie, while comforting Sophie, and even while changing Sophie's diaper. In fact, some of the best worship I have ever offered to my Lord happened in the wee hours of the morning while rocking my baby girl to sleep. Please Lord; continue to show me new ways to worship You. And no matter the situation or the circumstance, help me to always give You the glory and the honor You deserve.

Lesson Eight
God Loves Me

People always tell you that until you have a child of your own you cannot possibly understand the love that is involved. And you know what? They are right. I could not have imagined the love that I now feel for Sophie. I love Corey, but it is a different kind of love. This love is a protective, nurturing, wiping-running-noses-with-your-hand-if-necessary kind of love. It is a changing-the-bath-water-because-she-pooped-and-starting-the-process-all-over-again kind of love. And as my mother often warned me, it is a you-had-better-not-mess-with-my-kid kind of love. I used to lie in bed and plan my route of escape in case of a fire, intruder, natural disaster, etc. Now I lie in bed and plan my route for getting Sophie to safety. Your whole mind set changes, not instantly, but it changes because there is a new indescribable love present, and it is all consuming. Now, granted, what I am about to say next I have on very little authority because Sophie is currently only 10 months old. But, from what I can tell, any anger I am going to feel for her as she messes up or makes mistakes will be out of love. What I mean is this. Sophie is going to make some bad choices in the future, and that scares me because when you love someone this much, you do not want them to hurt or go through hard times. On a selfish note, I will also venture to guess that when Sophie hurts, Mommy and Daddy hurt. Therefore, any frustration or anger will most likely be the physical manifestation of all of my dreams, hopes, and love for her. Do you get where I am going with this?

I am such a flawed human specimen, but even in my poor attempt at unconditional love, I see how amazing God's love must truly be. He is my Father, and He loves me as His child. He hurts for me and wishes He could save me from myself sometimes. He has hopes and dreams for me, and He shakes His head with frustration when I make unwise decisions. I know sometimes He wants to pick me up, shake me, and say, "Don't you know who your Father is? We don't act that way in this family!" But God knows that pain and confusion are oftentimes the lessons I need most. So like a good Father, He does not swoop in and make every decision for me, but He is always waiting, good or bad, for me to come running home. God loves me. And you know what is really crazy? He loves me more than I love Sophie.

Lesson Nine
Maybe I'm Asking the Wrong Questions

I do not want what I am about to say to be misinterpreted as flippant or arrogant. It has taken a lot of time for me to come to grips with this fact, and I do not take it lightly. God is in control of everything. Now, if you are confused as to why I thought that idea might offend someone, then you are precisely where I was pre-colic. Allow me to explain. Pre-colic I had no problem saying God is in control of everything. "The colic," however, opened my eyes, as did parenthood in general. You see, it is easy to say God is in control of everything when everything is working out exactly the way you planned. The pill becomes a little harder to swallow when you throw in things that are not so pleasant, colic being the least of these. What about cancer? AIDS? Birth defects? Disabilities? Car crashes? Rape? Murder? The answer, God is in control of everything.

And that is when the light bulb came on for me. I do not need to understand why bad things happen to good people. I do not have to ask where was God when.... I do not need God to explain Himself to me. Bottom line, God is in control of everything. That is all I need to know. I have wasted far too much time asking the wrong questions. Why did God make colic? I do not know, but I do not have to. Why does God love me so much that He reaches out to me in any way He can? I do not know that either. Why does He give me chance after chance after chance? Couldn't tell you! All I know is that these are the questions with which I now choose to fill my mind. Why does God love me? How is God using this situation to help me? What really cool way will God's glory shine through this seemingly horrible situation? It is the new dialogue of my mind. God is in control. God loves His children. God wants all of us to be His children. If these are not the answers you are finding, you are probably asking the wrong questions.

Lesson Ten
Just Keep Running

I have always wanted to be a runner. I am not built like a runner, I do not particularly enjoy running, and I know running is bad for the joints, but I have still always wanted to be a runner. It took me a long time to figure out why, but I think I finally did. I have always wanted to be a runner because I firmly believe running to be 95% mental. I really believe that so much of it is endurance, and by that I mean mental endurance. That is why I have always wanted to be a runner. I believed that the only reason I was not a runner was because I was mentally weak, and that drove me crazy! I wanted to be able to go out and hit the open road with the belief that I could run and press on toward that goal until I completed a mile. Then I wanted to just add to that. Press on to 2 miles. Mentally run myself to 3 miles. Then 4, then 5, and so on and so on. Yet every time I would begin running, I would fail. I could not convince myself to keep going. Instead, I would spend the whole run thinking about how much everything hurt until I would finally just stop, not because my body said to but because my mind did. This went on literally for years. That is until I met "The Colic"!

I was unable to exercise for 6 weeks and did not start running again till week eight. For eight weeks, I battled all kinds of colic demons, the lies that I was doing something wrong and that I was a bad mother, the depression and the loneliness that come from being locked up in your house when you are used to always being on the go, the frustration and confusion of post surgery, a body I did not recognize, and motherhood, the struggle to pray when you have no idea what to pray for, not to mention, the strain such a life altering event puts on one's marriage. Day in and day out, I battled my little colic war with all its casualties. Day in and day out, I learned to rely on God. Day in and day out, I learned patience and all about a new found love for an unhappy little girl. Day in and day out, I had to look colic in the eye and say, "You are not bringing me down!" And through all of this, something was happening inside me. Something was changing, and I was not even aware.

I did not realize I was different until week eight. I went out for my first run in almost eleven months and ran for 26 minutes. Over the next few weeks, 27 minutes, 28, 30, 32! I would go running, and my whole mind set had changed. It was no longer, "Oh, my goodness, I can't make it another step!" It was now, "Oh, surely I can make it to the corner." Then I would reach the corner and think, "Surely I can make it to that next tree." And I would run, really run! I was becoming a runner, and that is the answer to it all. We just have to keep running! We can't focus on the pain. We can't let our minds dwell on the unpleasantness of the here and now. We have to focus on the prize and run the race that has been set out for each one of us. We just have to keep running! Sometimes it will feel good, and sometimes it won't. We just have to keep running! Sometimes the wind will be behind us, and sometimes it will be knocking us in the face. We just have to keep running!

I can now run 5 miles, and I am starting to train for a mini-marathon. But far more important, I have learned to be a runner for God. I do not want to ever stop. I do not want to ever quit. I want to just keep running until I see my Father and He says, "Well done, my good and faithful servant." Until then, regardless of the obstacles, I pray that God will give me the strength and endurance to just keep running!

Addendum

In the time between the writing and the publishing of this book, which for the record is five years, I have completed a marathon and a half marathon. I have also given birth to one of the most laid back little boys you will ever meet. I do not say this to brag, well maybe a little, but I say this as a reminder. All of us who have endured difficult times have come out on the other side different people. It is my hope and prayer that we learn to let God decide how our personalities will be changed by the not-so-pleasant moments. I pray that we let God determine who we will be when our time of testing is over. And in closing I will say this, the pre-colic Ronda dreamed of being a runner. The post-colic Ronda is a runner.